Wh
J

I.Q.?

What's Your JEWISH I.Q.?

*Test Yourself on Religion,
Literature,
the Arts,
and the World*

RABBI ALEX J. GOLDMAN

CITADEL PRESS
Kensington Publishing Corp.
www.kensingtonbooks.com

CITADEL PRESS BOOKS are published by

Kensington Publishing Corp.
850 Third Avenue
New York, NY 10022

All Kensington titles, imprints, and distributed lines are available at special quantity discounts for bulk purchases for sales promotions, premiums, fund-raising, educational, or institutional use. Special book excerpts or customized printings can also be created to fit specific needs. For details, write or phone the office of the Kensington special sales manager: Kensington Publishing Corp., 850 Third Avenue, New York, NY 10022, attn: Special Sales Department, phone 1-800-221-2647.

Citadel Press and the Citadel Logo are trademarks of Kensington Publishing Corp.

First printing: November 2001

10 9 8 7 6 5 4 3 2 1

Printed in the United States of America

Cataloging data may be obtained from the Library of Congress.

ISBN 0-8065-2005-1

To my wife, Edith,
my children, Dr. Robert Goldman and Richard
and Pamela Kesselman, and
my grandchildren, Steven and
Sarah Kesselman.

CONTENTS

PREFACE

If you lack knowledge, what do you have?
If you have knowledge, what do you lack?
—Levi. Ecclesiastes, 7:23

In other words, it's good to know. Knowing fulfills us, gives us vitality, and elicits respect and admiration from others. Understanding things makes one a more interesting human being.

For the Jewish people, through a turbulent five-millennia history of persecution, revolution, and exile, knowledge has meant even more than enlightenment—knowledge has meant survival. Through invasions, inquisitions, pogroms, and a Holocaust, Jews never stopped studying, and wisdom proved stronger than spears, fire, guns, tanks, and poison gas, as all of the enemies eventually fell while Jewish life continued. Descartes said, "I think, therefore I am." For the Jewish people, this famous quote has a poignant double meaning.

There are many ways to acquire knowledge and achieve understanding. Socrates favored a question-and-answer format, and we find the same method in Jewish history. *Responsa,* the literature that rabbis have used for hundreds of years to develop and adjust Jewish practice, is based on *Sh'aylot u'T'shuvot,* a tradition in which people would query their rabbis and the rabbis would study, analyze, evaluate, answer, and adjudicate. Thus, through questions and answers, Jewish law evolved and Jewish life was enriched.

In the tradition of *Sh'aylot u'T'shuvot,* this book will ask questions, and you will try your best to give answers. This is not an exam; there is no proctor, no time limit, and you won't need a No. 2 pencil. Have fun and see how much you know. Of course, the real joy lies in discovering what you don't know—and learning it. The answers provided at the back will give you all the facts and enhance your understanding of Jewish life in all its dimensions, from the synagogue to the street.

The great Hillel was once asked to explain all of Judaism while standing on one foot. He responded, "What is hateful to you, do not do unto others"—the well-known Golden Rule. He then added, *"Zil g'more,"* which means "Go and study." If this book inspires you to go and study, to find more answers, or even to ask more questions, then it will have achieved its purpose and provided the author with much satisfaction.

Rabbi Alex Goldman

Who is ashamed to ask will diminish in wisdom among men.

—Moses Ibn Ezra

Who is not ashamed to ask will in the end be exulted.

—Samuel B. Nahman

A man's question is half the answer.

—Ibn Gabirol

What's Your
JEWISH
I.Q.?

Questions

1.The Bible

1 What is the Bible?

2 How many sections comprise the Bible?

3 Name the sections.

4 What is the first section called and how many books does it contain?

5 Name the books.

6 Who are the Three Patriarchs of the Bible?

7 Who are the Four Matriarchs?

8 What are the two greatest events in the second book of Pentateuch?

9 What holiday is derived from Exodus?

10 In order, what are the Ten Commandments?

11 The Ten Commandments consist of two tablets. What is the difference between the two?

12 Name the three most famous kings in the Bible.

13 As a young man, who did King David vanquish with a slingshot?

14 What was King Solomon's most famous quality, and what did he build?

15 Which two books in the third section of the Bible are named after women?

16 Which book in the Bible is considered the greatest love story in history?

17 Which book is used mostly for prayers?

18 What sentence from the Bible is engraved on the Liberty Bell in Philadelphia?

19 What does written Torah mean?

20 What acronym is derived from the name of the Bible's three sections?

2. Founders

These men founded or strongly influenced famous Jewish institutions in America. Match the man to the organization.

1. Stephen Wise	a. Hebrew Union College
2. Henry Monsky	b. Anti-Defamation League
3. John Slawson	c. Jewish Institute of Religion
4. Simon Wolf	d. B'nai B'rith
5. Solomon Schechter	e. American Jewish Committee
6. Kaufmann Kohler	f. Jewish Theological Seminary
7. Bernard Revel	g. Board of Delegates of American Israelites
8. Richard Gutstadt	h. Yeshiva University

3. The Talmud

1 What is the Talmud?

2 The Bible is called Written Torah. Why is the Talmud known as the unwritten or Oral Torah?

3 What is the Talmud's other name?

4 How many tractates (books) comprise the Talmud?

5 What Rabbi of the Talmud said, "If I am not for myself, who will be for me? / If I care only for myself, what am I?

6 The Talmud had a great commentator without whom it would not be understood. Who was he?

4. Film

1 What filmmaker brought us *Jaws, E.T., Schindler's List,* and *Saving Private Ryan*?

2 Who was born Emmanuel Goldenberg in Bucharest, Romania, and grew up to become the quintessential gangster in Hollywood films?

3 What beautiful movie star converted to Judaism before marrying her third husband, playwright Arthur Miller?

4 What "divine" diva starred in *The Rose, Ruthless People,* and *Beaches*?

5 What actress won Oscars for her roles in *Butterfield 8* and *Who's Afraid of Virginia Woolf* and converted to Judaism before marrying her third husband?

6 What great character actor played the lead roles in *Emile Zola* and *Inherit the Wind*?

7 Name the beautiful actress who was born Betty Joan Persky and married the man with whom she costarred in her motion picture debut *To Have and Have Not*?

8 Anna Lifschutz left her shtetl in Minsk in 1905, escaping the pogrom massacres being committed against Russian Jews. Lucky for Hollywood, as her grandson became the biggest movie star of his generation, portraying such heroes as Indiana Jones and Han Solo. Who is he?

9 What young actress played an airhead with a good heart in *Clueless*, and Batgirl in *Batman Forever*?

5. Codes

1 What are the Codes?

2 Who is Moses Maimonides?

3 What is the Code of Maimonides?

4 What is the Code of Jewish Law?

5 What do the terms Shulchan Aruch and Mapat HaShulchan mean?

6. Words for the Law and Practice

Match words and meanings.

1.	Talmud Torah	a.	one who slaughters cattle or fowl
2.	halacha	b.	ten commandments
3.	shochet	c.	charity
4.	mitzvah	d.	ritually prepared
5.	aseret hadibrot	e.	fringes on garment
6.	tzitzit	f.	head covering
7.	kosher	g.	Jewish law
8.	bikkur cholim	h.	study of Torah/Hebrew school
9.	tzedakah	i.	a good deed/commandment
10.	kippa (yarmulka)	j.	mitzvah of visiting the sick

7. More Film

1 What movie actor starred in *Spartacus* and wrote a book about his father, *The Ragman's Son?*

2 What actress and singer got her Hollywood start in *Funny Girl* and became one of the most powerful figures in Hollywood?

3 Who starred with Humphrey Bogart in such classic films as *The Maltese Falcon* and *Casablanca?*

4 What film auteur, who always wears a pair of horn-rimmed glasses, is famous for directing, producing, writing, and starring in such films as *Annie Hall, Manhattan,* and *Husbands and Wives?*

5 What actor, whose daughter is also a film star, starred in *Houdini* and *The Count of Monte Crisco?*

6 Who is married to Phoebe Cates and acted in *Henry VI, The Pirates of Penzance,* and *A Fish Called Wanda?*

7 What cinematographer directed photography on such films as *Young Dillinger* and *The Three Faces of Eve?*

8 What film actor took Hollywood by storm in 1967 with his performance as Benjamin in *The Graduate?*

8. The Jewish Calendar

1 Is the Jewish calendar's division of months lunar (based on the cycle of the moon) or solar (based on the earlier belief in the revolution of the sun)?

2 From what literary source is the calendar derived?

3 How many months are there in the Jewish calendar?

4 Name the months in the Jewish calendar.

5 How often does a leap year occur in the Jewish calendar?

6 During a leap year, in what season is the addition to the year made?

7 What is the name of the Jewish leap month?

8 What is the Hebrew term for the first of the month?

9 According to the Jewish calendar, when does one day end and the next begin?

10 Five months of the Jewish calendar always have twenty-nine days, and five always have thirty. The remaining two months swing between twenty-nine and thirty days. Which two months are these?

9. Television

1 I was a famous baseball announcer, known as "The Voice of the Yankees." Who am I?

2 I played the title role in the television series *Molly Goldberg,* and I was known for my distinctive call to my neighbor, "Yoo, hoo, Mrs. Bloom!" Who am I?

3 I played an astute, cigar-chomping detective, always looking disheveled in a sloppy raincoat. Who am I?

4 I am the son of a Chicago cigar maker. I helped create the CBS network. Who am I?

5 My real name is Leonard Goldberg. I play Felix in the TV version of Neil Simon's *Odd Couple.* Who am I?

6 I am a famous comedian. My observational humor earned me $1 million per episode on my eponymous sit-com, which ended in 1998 after a nine-year run. Who am I?

10. Dates and Events

Match the dates with the events.

1. 1312 B.C.E.   a. Warsaw Ghetto uprising
2. 1014 B.C.E.   b. Creation of the modern state of Israel
3.   586 B.C.E.   c. Revolt of Bar Kochba against Rome
4.   516 B.C.E.   d. Building of the First Temple
5.   165 B.C.E.   e. Six-Day War
6.   70 C.E.   f. Expulsion of the Jews from Spain
7.   132 C.E.   g. The Exodus
8. 1492 C.E.   h. Destruction of the First Temple
9. 1654 C.E.   i. Balfour Declaration
10. 1917 C.E.   j. Completion of the Second Temple
11. 1938 C.E.   k. Fiftieth anniversary of the State of Israel
12. 1943 C.E.   l. Yom Kippur War
13. 1948 C.E.   m. *Kristallnacht*
14. 1967 C.E.   n. The Hanukkah story
15. 1973 C.E.   o. Destruction of the Second Temple
16. 1995 C.E.   p. Assassination of Yitzhak Rabin
17. 1998 C.E.   q. Jews arrive in America

11. Musicians

1 What great clarinet player got his instrument from a rabbi in Chicago?

2 What versatile actor, folksinger, and guitarist, who fled Nazi Germany, has produced many albums of Jewish and Hebrew melodies?

3 Who created *Porgy and Bess* and *Rhapsody in Blue?*

4 Who composed *Alexander's Ragtime Band* and *White Christmas?*

5 What famous singer was a cantor's son?

6 What singer established a woman's golf tournament and loved singing a song that ended with "finah"?

7 What émigré from Denmark was a piano player, comedian, humorist, and recitalist and was active in the Thanks to Scandinavia Scholarship Fund, which commemorates the Danish rescue of Jews from the Nazis in World War II?

8 What musical comedy star achieved success as Baron Münchausen?

9 What three-member Jewish band was the first white rap

group—and received the scorn of critics and strident hip-hop musicians for cultural pirating?

10 What multitalented musician won a Grammy in 1998 for *Fly* Away? (He later received another Grammy for his cover of *American Woman*.)

12. Common Phrases

Match words and meanings.

h 1. "l'chayim"   a. "so be it"

f 2. "shalom"   b. "happy holiday"

i 3. "gam zu l'tova"   c. "may he rest in peace"

a 4. "amen"   d. "happy new year"

g 5. "mazel tov"   e. "thank you"

j 6. "Shabbat shalom"   f. "hello"/"good-bye"

c 7. "alav hashalom"   g. "good luck"

d 8. "l'shana tova"   h. "to life"

e 9. "todah rabbah"   i. "this, too, is for good"

b 10. "chag samayach"   j. "good Sabbath"

13. Stage

1 Who was the first Tevye in *Fiddler on the Roof*?

2 Name the producer of *Sunday in the Park With George* and *Into the Woods*.

3 Who was known as the "Last of the Red Hot Mammas"?

4 Name an octogenarian actor who appeared in *The Godfather, Part III* and still performs on Broadway.

5 What great French actress of the nineteenth century was dubbed "The Divine Sarah" by Oscar Wilde?

6 Who starred in dramas like *The Dybbuk* and was the most renowned actor in Yiddish theater?

7 What former vaudeville star became one of America's best-loved actress/comediennes, the subject of three Hollywood films, and even had a federal postage stamp issued in her name?

8 What contemporary woman playwright wrote *The Heidi Chronicles*?

9 Who played the role of Otto Frank in the play *The Diary of Anne Frank*?

10 This playwright gained his first success with *All My Sons* in 1947. Who is he?

14. The Sabbath

1 When does the Sabbath occur?

2 Where is the Sabbath first mentioned in the Bible?

3 What does the word Sabbath mean?

4 What symbols are used on the Sabbath?

5 What is a mother's role on the Sabbath regarding candles?

6 What is the father's role regarding wine?

7 What special song welcomes the Sabbath?

8 What is the Sabbath greeting in Hebrew?

9 What is the Sabbath greeting in Yiddish?

10 How does the Sabbath begin?

11 What does *havdalah* mean?

12 What symbols are used during *havdalah*?

13 When does Sabbath begin, and when are the candles lit?

14 Why is there an interval between the onset of the Sabbath and the lighting of the candles?

15 Why are two candles lit on the Sabbath?

15. Words for the Sabbath

Match words and meanings.

1. challah

    a. halachic device used to allow people to carry in public on Sabbath

2. oneg Shabbat

    b. Sabbath songs

3. shalosh s'udot

    c. spices used for havdalah

4. zemirot

    d. ceremony performed at the end of Sabbath to separate it from the rest of the week

5. kiddush   e. long-simmered stew traditionally
                         served for Sabbath meal

6. erev shabbat   f. Sabbath enjoyment

7. havdalah   g. blessing made over wine at the
                         beginning of Sabbath meal

8. besamim   h. three Sabbath meals (techni-
                         cally, the third meal, Sabbath
                         afternoon)

9. eruv   i. Sabbath eve

10. cholent   j. braided bread

16. Comedy

1 What banjo-eyed entertainer became a millionaire star-ring in the *Ziegfeld Follies,* lost all his money in the Wall Street crash of 1929, and then rebounded to become one of America's most popular authors, radio entertainers, and film stars?

2 What comedian started in vaudeville, ended up on tele-vision, and is best known for his penny-pinching jokes and his violin?

3 What five-brother Broadway vaudeville act achieved stardom as a four-man, and later as a three-man, slap-stick comedy team?

4 What cigar-smoking comedian played God—literally—and made it to age one hundred?

5 Name the TV and film star who was once Dean Martin's partner in comedy and now conducts an annual round-the-clock Labor Day telethon for Muscular Dystrophy.

6 "I get no respect!" is the mantra of what Jewish comedian?

7 What Emmy-award winning comic legend cowrote and costarred in television's *Your Show of Shows*? (He also received the National Foundation for Jewish Culture's Second Annual Alan King Award in American Jewish Humor.)

8 What husband and wife team performed more than thirty times on the *Ed Sullivan Show*?

9 What writer for Sid Caesar went on to write for the movies, turning out the hits *Young Frankenstein, Blazing Saddles,* and *The Producers*?

10 What comedian got his start in the Borscht Belt, became a member of the Rat Pack, and had his own television show under his own name?

11 I was a popular comedian and host, known as Toastmaster General of the United States. Who am I?

12 I started acting at five and became the best-known actress and comedienne in the history of Yiddish theater. Who am I?

13 Many couldn't stomach my obscene humor, but others found it revolutionary—and hilarious. A movie was made about me, but if I told you what it was called, you'd know my first name. Who am I?

14 I starred in musical comedies and achieved fame playing Baron Münchausen. Who am I?

15 I am known simply as "The Master of Mime." Who am I?

17. Birth

1 What does "Shalom Zachar" mean?

2 When is "Shalom Zachar" celebrated?

3 What does brit mean?

4 On what day is a baby circumcised?

5 What is a Mohel?

6 When is a boy given his Hebrew name?

7 When and where is a little girl named?

8 What occurs in the ceremony called Pidyon HaBen?

18. Funnymen

Who said?

1 "I would never belong to any club that would have me as a member."

    a. Woody Allen
    b. Groucho Marx
    c. Eddie Cantor

2 "Edgar Bergen was a ventriloquist *on the radio*! How do we know he wasn't moving his lips?"

    a. Robert Klein
    b. Jackie Mason
    c. Jerry Seinfeld

3 "When a couple of his goons were beating me to death, Frank Sinatra saved my life with two words: 'That's enough.'"

    a. George Burns
    b. Jack Benny
    c. Shecky Greene

4 "The only things I believe in are sex and death. But at least after death you're not nauseous."

    a. Woody Allen
    b. Joan Rivers
    c. Jerry Lewis

5 To the manager of a restricted country club: "My daughter's only half Jewish. Can she go into the pool up to her knees?"

    a. George Jessel
    b. Phil Silvers
    c. Groucho Marx

6 Said after the Six-Day War: "I'm going to Israel to visit the Pyramids!"

    a. Henny Youngman
    b. Joan Rivers
    c. Frank Sinatra

7 "Jews prove their optimistic nature by cutting a quarter-inch off the penis before they even know how long it's going to be."

    a. Jerry Seinfeld
    b. Jackie Mason
    c. Carl Reiner

8 "Insanity is hereditary—you can get it from your children."

    a. Groucho Marx
    b. Al Jolson
    c. Eddie Cantor

9 "A lousy businessman is one who goes bankrupt and doesn't make a cent either time."

    a. Alan King
    b. Myron Cohen
    c. George Burns

10 "When a Jew doesn't care for something, he says, 'It's not my glass of tea.'"

    a. Mel Brooks
    b. Woody Allen
    c. Molly Picon

19. Words for Life Cycle Events

Match words and meanings.

1.	ketubah	a.	matchmaker
2.	pidyon haben	b.	bride
3.	ufruf	c.	divorce
4.	chatan (chasan)	d.	festive occasion/celebration
5.	mohel	e.	party to welcome a baby boy
6.	le'vayah	f.	gathering in honor of the bride on the Sabbath before the wedding
7.	mishpacha	g.	seven-day period of mourning
8.	shadchan	h.	marriage document
9.	get	i.	groom
10.	shiva	j.	funeral
11.	chatuna	k.	special aliyah (Torah honor) for groom on the Sabbath before the wedding
12.	shalom zachar	l.	redemption of the firstborn son
13.	kallah	m.	one who performs circumcision
14.	simcha	n.	family
15.	Shabbat Kallah	o.	wedding ceremony

20. Composers

Match the composer to his composition.

1.	Giocomo Meyerbeer	a.	*Kaddish*
2.	Sigmund Romberg	b.	*The Cradle Will Rock*
3.	Gustav Mahler	c.	*Sweeney Todd*
4.	Aaron Copland	d.	*Show Boat*
5.	Leonard Bernstein	e.	*Oklahoma!*
6.	Marc Blitzstein	f.	*The Chocolate Soldier*
7.	Richard Rodgers	g.	*Advodat Hakodesh*
8.	George Gershwin	h.	*Verklaerte Nacht*
9.	Kurt Weil	i.	*Appalachian Spring*
10.	Jerome Kern	j.	*The Student Prince*
11.	Oscar Strauss	k.	*La Juive*
12.	Stephen Sondheim	l.	*Rhapsody in Blue*
13.	Arnold Schoenberg	m.	*The Eternal Road*
14.	Ernest Bloch	n.	*L'Africaine*
15.	François Halévy	o.	*Das Lied von der Erde*

21. Bar Mitzvah

1 What is a bar mitzvah?

2 What does bar mitzvah mean?

3 When is a boy bar mitzvah?

4 What is he expected to do?

5 What is a bat/bas mitzvah?

6 What does bat/bas mitzvah mean?

7 When is a girl bat/bas mitzvah?

8 What is the difference between *bas* and *bat*?

9 Does a girl have the same duties as a bar mitzvah?

22. Sports

1 I was the first Jew elected to Baseball's Hall of Fame. As a Detroit Tiger I slugged fifty-eight home runs in one

season, only two shy of Babe Ruth's then-record total. In the World Series I played on Rosh Hashanah—but not on Yom Kippur. Who am I?

2 I was a clever and courageous boxer, and became lightweight and welterweight champion of the world. I received the Silver Star and Distinguished Service Cross for service in the Second World War, and they even made a movie about me, *Monkey on My Back*. Who am I?

3 Many consider me the greatest pitcher who ever stood on a mound. As a Brooklyn Dodger, I pitched four no-hitters in four seasons and one perfect game, and I beat Christy Mathewson's 1902 strikeout record. Who am I?

4 My name is on the list of the National Football League's Most Valuable Players, the Pro Football Hall of Fame, and the Jewish Sports Hall of Fame. I was a passer, runner, blocker, kicker, and tackler. The famous "T formation," now common in football, was my personal innovation. Who am I?

5 I am from Orange, New Jersey, and I was a tennis star. In 1951 I defeated Ken McGregor of Australia at Wimbledon. Who am I?

6 I shattered world records as a swimmer for the United States, winning seven gold medals at the 1972 Olympic Games. Who am I?

7 We were two of the fastest runners in the world and destined for gold medals when we were prevented from running in the so-called Nazi Olympics in Berlin in 1936. Who are we?

8 My brother and I fought Joe Louis three times and we lost every fight. But I was world heavyweight champion in 1934. Who am I? And who was my brother? And who did I knock out to become champion?

9 In the 1920s I played second base for the New York Giants, succeeding Rogers Hornsby. I was one of the first Jewish baseball players to play under my own name. Who am I?

10 I ran and I ran, and I became famous for running one of New York City's great annual sports events. Who am I?

23. Confirmation

1 What is Confirmation?

2 When did the ceremony enter Judaism?

3 To what holiday is it attached?

4 Do all Jews observe Confirmation?

5 What are some of the customs of the service?

24. Words for the Temple

Match words and meanings.

1.	bet tefillah	a.	Torah honor
2.	maftir	b.	Torah reader
3.	chatan Torah	c.	priest
4.	parochet	d.	last Torah honor
5.	chazzan	e.	synagogue as house of prayer
6.	gabbai	f.	cantor
7.	keter Torah	g.	synagogue as house of assembly
8.	baal tefillah	h.	breast plate of Torah
9.	yad	i.	crown of Torah
10.	aliyah	j.	prayer shawl
11.	talit	k.	Torah pointer
12.	chatan b'rayshit	l.	one who leads services

13. baal k'riah   m. first honor of Torah on Simchat
                            Torah

14. mechitzah   n. last honor of Torah on Simchat
                            Torah

15. etz chaim   o. tree of life (Torah wooden
                            rollers)

16. choshen   p. synagogue official

17. bimah   q. ark covering

18. rav   r. dais/pulpit

19. bet k'nesset   s. separation (used to separate
                            women's section from men's)

20. cohen/cohayn   t. rabbi

25. Marriage

1 What is the Hebrew word for wedding?

2 What is the Hebrew word for bridegroom?

3 What is the Hebrew word for bride?

4 What is a *chuppah?*

5 What does the *chuppah* symbolize?

6 How many cups of wine are used in the wedding ceremony?

7 What is the rationale for the number of cups?

8 How many rings are used?

9 What is the one provision for the rings?

10 On what finger does a groom place the ring?

11 Can a groom give a broach instead of a ring?

12 What is *ketubah?*

13 What does *Shevah Brachot* mean?

14 Who breaks the glass at the end of the ceremony?

15 What well-known two-word Hebrew phrase do family and friends declare when the ceremony is over?

26. More Sports

1 What Jewish woman from Philadelphia achieved more than one perfect 300 in bowling?

2 What lightweight boxing champion from New York's Lower East Side was considered the world's best pound-for-pound fighter during his title reign in the twenties, and retired because his Yiddish-speaking mother was afraid he'd get hurt?

3 What Ping-Pong player from Hungary won twenty-two world titles and is considered the greatest in history?

4 What unusual baseball player for the White Sox mastered nine languages, allegedly worked for the CIA, and is considered the most intelligent baseball player ever?

5 What Jewish three-time Olympian, four-time Maccabiah games gold medalist, and winner of forty-two world titles, was recently inducted into the National Track and Field Hall of Fame?

27. Funerals

1 How soon after death does the funeral take place?

2 What are *Shomrim?*

3 Why is a person buried in a plain box (no elaborate coffin) and a shroud?

4 Why do we wash our hands after leaving the cemetery?

5 Why do mourners eat an egg after the funeral?

6 What does it mean to "sit shiva"?

7 Who is required to sit shiva?

8 What are the symbols of mourning?

9 What is *Kaddish?*

10 What is a *Yortzeit?*

11 How long does the extended period of mourning last?

12 When is the tombstone placed on the gravesite?

13 What is placed on the tombstone when visiting the grave, instead of flowers?

28. Hall-of-Famers

Match these Hall-of-Famers with their sports.

1. Benny Friedman   a. Basketball
2. Red (Arnold) Auerbach   b. Football
3. Lillian Copeland   c. Speed skating
4. Marshall Goldberg   d. Auto racing
5. Nat Holman   e. Horse racing
6. Irving Jaffee   f. Bullfighting
7. Harry Litwack   g. Track and field
8. Walter Miller   h. Fencing
9. Myer Prinstein   i. Wrestling
10. Henry B. Wittenberg   j. Boxing
11. Sidney Franklin
12. Endre Kabos
13. Sid Luckman
14. Mauri Rose
15. Harold Abrahams

29. Fast Days

1 What is the most important fast day in the Jewish faith?

2 How long does the fasting last?

3 Can you name another fast day that begins at night and goes through the next day?

4 What fast day is connected to a beautiful woman?

5 Which fast day relates to Purim?

6 Which fast day relates to Passover?

7 Which fast day commemorates the destruction of the First and Second Temple?

8 Match the names of these fast days with their descriptions:

a. Shiva Asar B'Tammuz   1. Tenth day of Tevet
b. Tzom Gedaliah   2. Seventeenth day of Tammuz
c. Asarah B'Tevet   3. Fast of Gedaliah

30. Rosh Hashanah

1 What is Rosh Hashanah, and when is it celebrated?

2 Where in the Bible is Rosh Hashanah mentioned?

3 What is another name for Rosh Hashanah in the Bible?

4 What is the difference between the challah of Sabbath and the challah of Rosh Hashanah?

5 What is the shofar?

6 Where in the Bible is the shofar introduced?

7 Who blows the shofar at the rabbi's prompting?

8 What are the names of the sounds of the shofar?

9 How many sounds are blown each day of Rosh Hashanah?

10 What is *tashlich?*

31. Words for Prayer

Match words and meanings.

1.	Maariv	a.	blessing
2.	Kaddish	b.	memorial prayer said on holidays
3.	siddur	c.	blessing said over bread
4.	birkat hamazon	d.	blessing at Torah meaning "may He who blessed"
5.	shma yisrael	e.	shma on parchment affixed to doorpost
6.	hakafot	f.	afternoon service
7.	bracha	g.	quorum of ten for prayer
8.	tephilin	h.	Torah reading
9.	Shachrit	i.	mourner's prayer
10.	hamotzee	j.	daily prayerbook
11.	Yiskor	k.	evening service
12.	mezuzah	l.	Torah portion of the week
13.	k'ree-at haTorah	m.	grace after meals
14.	sidra	n.	phylacteries for head and arm
15.	mi shehbayrach	o.	circuits (torah or lulav) in synagogue on Sukkot
16.	tehilim	p.	blessing meaning, "who has given us life"
17.	minyan	q.	"Hear, O Israel"

18. shehecheyanu   r.   prayer introducing Yom Kippur
                         Eve
19. Kol Nidre   s.   morning service
20. mincha   t.   psalms

32. Yom Kippur

1 What is Yom Kippur?

2 What is the connection between Yom Kippur and Rosh Hashanah?

3 Why does fasting occur on Yom Kippur?

4 What other name is Yom Kippur called in the Bible?

5 What is Kol Nidre?

6 What is the name of the last service of Yom Kippur?

7 When is the shofar blown on Yom Kippur?

8 What is said after the shofar is blown?

9 On what other occasion are the same words declared?

33. Authors

Match these authors to the titles of their works.

1. *Peace of Mind*   a. Howard Fast
2. *The Promised Land*   b. Erica Jong
3. *Dinner at Eight*   c. Joshua Roth
                                                      Liebman
4. *The Chosen*   d. Sholom Asch
5. *Portnoy's Complaint*   e. Edna Ferber
6. *My Glorious Brothers*   f. Jerome Weidman
7. *The Caine Mutiny*   g. Letty Cottin
                                                      Pogrebin
8. *Deborah, Golda, and Me*   h. Philip Roth
9. *The Young Lions*   i. Erich Siegel
10. *Exodus*   j. Mary Antin
11. *I Can Get It for You Wholesale* k. Chaim Potok
12. *Gentleman's Agreement*   l. Leon Uris
13. *Fear of Flying*   m. Irwin Shaw
14. *Love Story*   n. Herman Wouk
15. *The Nazarene*   o. Laura Z. Hobson

34. Sukkot

1 What is Sukkot?

2 When does the celebration of Sukkot begin?

3 For how many days is Sukkot celebrated?

4 What other name is the holiday called?

5 What is the *sukkah?*

6 What special symbols are used on Sukkot?

7 What do we do with these symbols?

8 What special meanings are usually attributed to these symbols?

9 What are the names of the last two days of Sukkot?

10 How is Simchat Torah celebrated?

35. Words for Holidays

Match words and meanings.

1.	afikomen	a.	high holy days
2.	Chanukah	b.	sending of gifts
3.	lulav	c.	willows of the brook
4.	tashlich	d.	searching for chametz
5.	yom tov	e.	myrtle branches
6.	chametz	f.	candelabra
7.	etrog	g.	unleavened bread
8.	menorah	h.	prayer book for the holidays
9.	aravot	i.	holiday/festival (literally "good day")
10.	bedikat chametz	j.	leavened bread
11.	mishloach manot	k.	casting sins in the river on first day of Rosh Hashanah
12.	hadasim	l.	festival of lights
13.	machzor	m.	date palm branch
14.	yamin norahim	n.	seder dessert
15.	matzoh	o.	citron

36. More Authors

1 What novelist, critic, and translator wrote *The Pagan Rabbi*?

2 The famous sonnet on the tablet held by the Statue of Liberty begins "Give us your tired, your poor . . ." Who wrote it?

3 What Jewish novelist wrote *Compulsion,* the story of the Leopold-Loeb murder case in Chicago?

4 What author, originally from Germany, wrote *The Island Within*?

5 What Nobel Prize-winning novelist, an Israeli, wrote *The Bridal Canopy*?

6 What professor at Notre Dame University and writer of more than twenty novels wrote the story of an eight-year-old boy growing up in Brooklyn?

7 What great Yiddish writer, known as "the storyteller," received the Nobel Prize for Literature in 1970?

8 The author from the previous question had a brother, also a renowned writer, who wrote *The Brothers Ashkenazi, East of Eden,* and the play *Yoshe Kalb.* What's his name?

9 This Yiddish writer, known as the father of Yiddish literature and the Jewish Mark Twain, has a pen name that is Hebrew for "peace be to you," "how are you," "hello," and "good-bye." Who is he?

10 This novelist is most associated with the city of Chicago. He wrote *The Adventures of Augie March, Herzog,* and *Henderson the Rain King?* He is?

11 Name the blessed young heroine in World War II whose poem "Blessed is the Match" became a rallying cry for resistance.

12 Who wrote *The Assistant?*

13 Who is the author of *When Bad Things Happen to Good People?*

37. Hanukkah

1 What is Hanukkah?

2 When is it celebrated and for how many days?

3 Why do we celebrate Hanukkah for this many days?

4 What are other names for Hanukkah?

5 Who are the following characters associated with Hanuk-kah?

     a. Mattathias
     b. Antiochus
     c. Judah Maccabee
     d. Simeon
     e. Hannah

6 What does Maccabee mean?

7 What is the menorah?

8 What is the purpose of the *shamesh* candle?

9 What is the dreidel?

10 Name the food that is synonymous with the celebration of Hanukkah.

38. Artists

1 I am a prolific artist of the twentieth century. I created stained-glass windows of the Twelve Tribes in the Hadassah Hospital chapel, Jerusalem, and the Rockefeller private chapel in Tarrytown, New York. My most famous painting is *I and the Village*. Who am I?

2 My most famous painting is *Praying on the Day of Atonement*. I am considered one of the leading artists of the nineteenth century. Who am I?

3 I had a passion for art and the Judaism of Hasidism. A special museum in Haifa houses many of my works. My first name was Emanuel before I changed it. Who am I?

4 I was a Jewish-Italian artist. Though I am considered to be among the greatest artists of the twentieth century, I had only one art exhibition and died at the age of thirty-six. Women with elongated faces, small piercing eyes, tight lips, and long angular necks mark my unique paintings. Who am I?

5 I was born into a Sephardic family in St. Thomas, Virgin Islands, and many considered me the "Father of Impressionism." I considered myself an anarchist. My work is known for huge landscapes . . . and I had a very long beard. Who am I?

6 I am known as "the Paul Gauguin of Israel," because I was born in Romania and emigrated to Palestine. I was later made ambassador to Romania. My first name sounds just like my surname. Who am I?

7 I was a colorful folklorist, artist, scribe, silversmith, stonemason, and watchmaker. I turned to whimsical creation of wooden toys. I started carving at seventy. I took the Hebrew word for "peace" as my fist name, and attached to it the Israeli town where I lived. Who am I?

8 I was a painter, photographer, and muralist. I loved the Hebrew alphabet and combined Hebrew letters with strong social themes, especially from the book of Ecclesiastes. I was selected over four hundred other artists to paint the mural for the Social Security Administration building in Washington, D.C. Who am I?

9 I am one of three brothers—all artists—who came to America in 1912 and painted average people and their suffering during the Depression. I always painted myself into my painting's theme. Who am I?

10 I am an Expressionist who painted with a violent, sweeping brush. I created paintings that dealt with food and slaughtered, disjointed animals, like *Hanging Turkey* and *Flayed Oxen.* My portrait subjects are often portrayed in exaggerated poses. Who am I?

11 I am considered one of the greatest illustrators, alphabetists, miniaturists, caricaturists, cartoonists, and calligraphers in history. My Hagaddah is one of my trademarks; my Declaration of Independence is another. Who am I?

12 I was born into the upper class. My work came from the upper classes and dominated the German art world for four decades. Later in life I became president of the Berlin Academy of Art—until the Nazis took over. Who am I?

13 I was fascinated by the free-spirited Isidora Duncan and painted freedom of movement and expression. My last name is similar to a major Jewish town in Poland. The Brooklyn Museum had an exhibition called "One Hundred Artists and [my name]." Who am I?

14 I was an Orthodox artist. I emphasized Jewish action in dance, prayer, and hand. I was also a woodcutter, printmaker, sculptor, writer, poet, and teacher. I died in 1961 in Great Neck, New York. Who am I?

15 My original name was Yitzhak Leiza. My *Washington Crossing the Delaware* is in the Museum of Modern Art. I started as a saxophonist. I've been called an iconoclastic artist because of my explicit paintings. Who am I?

39. Tu B'Shevat

1 What is Tu B'Shevat?

2 What does "Tu B'Shevat" mean?

3 Why is the "Tu" used?

4 What are some of the other names for this holiday?

5 How old is this holiday?

6 What customs are observed on this day?

7 How do Ashkenazi Jews celebrate it?

8 How do Sephardic Jews celebrate it?

40. Sculptors

1 Who is the most famous sculptor in Israel?

2 What famous Jewish sculptor, born on the Lower East Side of New York, was knighted by the Queen of England?

3 What familiar white-haired figure on the New York art scene whose first name means "life," sculpted in wood and specialized in bronze menorahs?

4 This sculptor was a prolific and intense worker who used the Bible as a source of deep expression. Among his creations are *David and Goliath, Jacob Wrestling with the Angel,* and *The Miracle Celebrating Israel.* His sculptures stand in the Guggenheim Museum and the Museum of Modern Art in New York.

5 A plaza near the World Trade Center in New York honors a great American woman sculptor. Who is she?

6 You can see my sculpture *The Destroyed City* in Rotterdam. Some say it was my greatest work. I was born in Russia and spent most of my years in Paris. Who am I?

7 This American-born sculptor was known primarily for his busts of prominent persons—from Franklin D. Roosevelt to Gertrude Stein. His famous statue of Walt Whitman stands in New York's Bear Mountain Park. Who was he?

8 This sculptor takes seriously the commandment against making graven images, but his dynamic sculptures are famous around the world. They can be seen especially in Israel and in France. Who is he?

41. Scientists

1 Who is commonly regarded as the greatest scientist ever?

2 As a chemist, he aided the British war effort in the First World War by producing massive quantities of acetone. Who was he, and what did he later become?

3 Who is the "father of psychoanalysis?"

4 Who was the great bridge builder responsible for the Mackinac Bridge, the Triborough Bridge, the Kingston Bridge, and nearly four hundred others?

5 Name the famous archaeologist who unearthed areas around the Western Wall in Jerusalem.

6 Who is known as the "father of the nuclear navy" for his development of the world's first nuclear submarine?

7 Which Israeli archaeologist gained renown for his excavations at Masada?

8 Called the most influential sociologist of his time, this man founded *L'Anne sociologique* but is perhaps best remembered for his study of suicide. Who is he?

9 Whose experiments with light disposed of the concept of the ether?

10 What distinguished physicist supervised the making of the atomic bomb?

42. Purim

1 What is Purim?

2 What does "Purim" mean?

3 What is the source for the story?

4 How is Purim celebrated in the synagogue?

5 How is Purim celebrated at home?

6 What special noisemaker is used on Purim?

7 Identify these characters from the story of Purim:

      a. Ahasuerus
      b. Vashti

c. Haman

d. Bigthan and Teresh

e. Mordecai

f. Zeresh

g. Esther

8 What do hamantaschen symbolize?

43. More Scientists

1 Who was a pioneer in the production of penicillin?

2 What scientist is known as the first electrical engineer in the world?

3 Who isolated the nutrients necessary for life and called them vitamins?

4 Who was known as the "Father of American Television" and also gained fame as the wireless operator who heard the call for help from the *Titanic*?

5 What physicist escaped from Europe before World War II and helped build the atomic bomb in America?

6 What atomic scientist received the Nobel Prize for Physics in 1944?

7 Who discovered DNA, the substance containing genetic material?

8 What member of a famous Jewish humanitarian family was one of the first to voice warnings that cigarette smoking is dangerous?

9 Who discovered the polio vaccine that now bears his name?

10 What Nobel physicist demonstrated with a simple experiment why the *Challenger* space shuttle exploded?

44. Passover

1 What is Passover?

2 When is it celebrated?

3 For how many days is it celebrated?

4 Name four customs that are observed in anticipation of Passover.

5 What are three other names by which Passover is known?

6 What is the significance of matzoh in the Passover celebration?

7 What does "Seder" mean?

8 What is the name of the book used at the Seder?

9 How many cups of wine do we drink during the Seder?

10 What do the three pieces of matzoh placed together represent?

11 What is the aphikomon?

12 How many times is Moses mentioned in the traditional Hagaddah?

13 For whom is the door opened and a special wine goblet is filled?

45. Passover Terms

Match these Passover terms with their meanings.

1. charoset   a. song, "It is enough"
2. baytzah   b. horseradish
3. dayaynu   c. wine, apples, and cinnamon
                     mixed together
4. chad gadyah   d. egg in Seder plate
5. maror   e. song, "One Goat"

46. Israel

1 I was the first prime minister of Israel. Who am I?

2 I was born and raised in South Africa, and I'm known as one of the greatest orators in history. I was Israel's ambassador to the United States and the United Nations. Who am I?

3 I was a pioneering Zionist, and advocated fighting for a Jewish state, with military force if necessary. I influenced Menachem Begin, Yitzhak Shamir, Benjamin Netanyahu, and many others. I died in 1940, and my remains were reinterred on Mount Herzl in Jerusalem in 1965. Who am I?

4 When the British Government appointed me High Commissioner for Palestine in 1921, I became the first Jew to govern in Israel in over two thousand years. Who am I?

5 I was a diplomat in Tunis in the early nineteenth century. I moved to New York and became an editor, lawyer, judge, and playwright. I believed in Zionism long before it was popular and tried to establish a Jewish State in Niagara Falls, New York. When I died in 1851, I was the most famous Jew in America. Who am I?

6 I was a stateswoman. I was born in Kiev and grew up in Milwaukee, Wisconsin, before settling in Palestine in 1921. I became the first, and so far the only, woman to be elected prime minister of Israel. Who am I?

7 I was Prime Minister of Israel in two different decades. Formerly the chief of staff of the Israeli military, I was the architect of Israel's victory in the Six Day War. I won the Nobel Peace Prize in 1994, and one year later I was assassinated. Who am I?

8 I was a tall, handsome, black-bearded Austrian jounalist. Today I am known as the "Father of Zionism." In 1897 I published *Der Judenstaat* (The Jewish State) in which I called for the establishment of a modern Jewish nation. Who am I?

9 I was a chemist, and I gave Britain a formula that helped the Allies win World War I. When the modern State of Israel was established, I was chosen to be its first president. Who am I?

10 I served in the U.S. Army in World War II and served with the prosecution at the Nuremberg war-crime trials. I became the most prominent of American volunteers to help organize the Israeli defense forces in 1948. Who am I?

47. Words for Israel

Match words and meanings.

1.	aliyah	a.	zion
2.	chalutz	b.	native born of Israel
3.	Yisrael	c.	Jerusalem
4.	Eretz Yisrael	d.	moving (going up) to Israel

5. galut   e. land of Israel
6. tziyon   f. western wall
7. haganah   g. Diaspora (outside Israel)
8. sabra   h. pioneer
9. Yerushalayim   i. Israel/prince of God
10. kotel   j. defense army of Israel

48. Shavuot

1 What is Shavuot?

2 What does "Shavuot" mean?

3 When is Shavuot celebrated?

4 For how many days is Shavuot celebrated?

5 What is the Hebrew term for the Counting of Weeks?

6 By what other names does the Bible refer to Shavuot?

7 What special nocturnal tradition takes place during Shavuot?

8 What excerpt of the Torah is read during the festival?

9 Which book of the Bible is read during the service?

10 What kind of foods are prepared for Shavuot?

49. United States Supreme Court

1 I was the first Jew ever to be appointed to the Supreme Court and was known as "The Great Dissenter." Who am I?

2 I was a Sephardic Jew and President Hoover appointed me to the Supreme Court to succeed Oliver Wendell Holmes. I wrote *The Nature of the Judicial Process* and other books that are considered classics of law literature. Who am I?

3 I was appointed to the Supreme Court by President Lyndon B. Johnson and was active in civil and human rights issues. Controversy over a private donation forced me to become the first Supreme Court justice to resign. Who am I?

4 I was a labor lawyer and the general counsel for the United Steelworkers of America. When President Kennedy appointed me to the Supreme Court, I helped to ad-

vance minority rights and raise the minimum wage. Who
am I?

5 President Roosevelt gave me the Supreme Court seat
formerly held by Justice Cardozo. I was a proponent of
judicial restraint; I believed that the people, through the
legislation of the officials they elect, should share the
laws they live by. Who am I?

6 Born in Brooklyn, I became the first Jewish woman ever
appointed to the Supreme Court. I am also the wealthiest
of all the justices, with a declared net worth of over $6
million. Who am I?

50. Lag B'Omer

1 What is Lag B'Omer?

2 What does "Lag B'Omer" mean and when does it
occur?

3 How is it celebrated?

4 What is the day's connection with weddings?

5 What is another name for Lag B'Omer?

51. Political Figures

1 I rose from poverty to become a Wall Street legend and an adviser to presidents. It was said that my office was a park bench near the White House. Who am I?

2 I helped organize the World Jewish Congress in 1936 and later served as its president. I was instrumental in securing reparations from Germany for survivors of the Holocaust. Who am I?

3 I left my mother's cosmetics business in 1973 to become a leader in the Jewish world and a media mogul. I helped finance the revitalization of Polish Jewry and became president of the Jewish National Fund. Who am I?

4 I am the chairman of Seagram Company Ltd. I am also president of the World Jewish Congress. Most recently, I have supported the cause of Holocaust survivors seeking reparations from Swiss banks that accepted, then hid and used monetary deposits from Holocaust victims. Who am I?

5 I was elected governor of New York State in 1932 and later headed UNRRA, the United Nations agency that worked for the poor and disenfranchised during World War II. In New York City there is a college named after me. Who am I?

6 I was secretary of the treasury under President Franklin D. Roosevelt, and I helped him institute his New Deal. Who am I?

7 My family escaped Nazi Germany. When President Richard M. Nixon appointed me secretary of state in 1973, I became the first Jew ever to hold that office. Who am I?

8 I was born in Russia in 1898 and returned there as an Israeli diplomat forty years after emigrating to the United States. Who am I?

9 I was the secretary of commerce and labor under Theodore Roosevelt, thereby becoming the first Jew to serve in a United States presidential cabinet. Who am I?

10 When I was elected to the Senate, I became the first professing Jew to serve there. Later, when the Confederate States of America was formed, I served in the cabinet of Jefferson Davis. Who am I?

52. Miscellaneous Words

Match words and meanings.

1.	chai	a.	study partner
2.	shaddai	b.	star of David
3.	nachat (nachas)	c.	contraction of three parts of the bible: T (Torah), N (Nevi'im), Kh (Ketuvim)
4.	tzaddik	d.	ordination of a rabbi
5.	ashkenazi	e.	Almighty
6.	bet midrash	f.	Torah scribe
7.	magen David	g.	god
8.	Chassid	h.	wisdom
9.	sofayr	i.	delight/happiness
10.	chavrusah	j.	children of the covenant
11.	semicha	k.	house of study
12.	chutzpah	l.	wise man
13.	adonai (adoshem)	m.	Hebrew alphabet
14.	sephardi	n.	nerve/audacity
15.	chochma	o.	Jew of Germanic/Polish origin
16.	ivrit	p.	a righteous/pious man
17.	TaNaCH	q.	one of a pious group

18. alef-bet   r.   Jew of Spanish origin
19. b'nai b'rith   s.   Hebrew language
20. chacham   t.   life

1. The Bible

1 The religious story of the Jewish People.

2 Three

3 Pentateuch (Five Books of Moses), Prophets, and Writings.

4 The Pentateuch has five books.

5 Genesis, Exodus, Leviticus, Numbers, and Deuteronomy.

6 Abraham, Isaac, and Jacob.

7 Sarah, Rebecca, Rachel, and Leah.

8 The Exodus and Giving of the Ten Commandments to Moses.

9 Passover

10 The Ten Commandments in order are:

   1. I am the Lord your God.

   2. You shall have no other gods before me.

   3. You shall not take the name of the Lord your God in vain.

   4. Observe the Sabbath day.

   5. Honor your father and your mother.

   6. You shall not murder.

   7. You shall not commit adultery.

   8. You shall not steal.

   9. You shall not bear false witness.

10. You shall not covet.

11 The first tablet contains the commandments between God and man; the second contains those between man and man.

12 Saul, David, Solomon.

13 Goliath

14 His wisdom, and he built the First Temple in Jerusalem.

15 Book of Esther and Book of Ruth.

16 Song of Songs.

17 The Psalms.

18 "Proclaim liberty throughout the land unto all the inhabitants thereof." (Leviticus 25:10)

19 Written Torah means the Torah written by Moses.

20 Tanakh, from Torah, Nevi'm (Prophets), Kethuvim (Writings).

2. Founders

1 c

2 d

3 e

4 g

5 f

6 a

7 h

8 b

3. The Talmud

1 A series of books, written after the Bible was finished, containing Jewish laws, practices, traditions and observances. (100 B.C.E.–500 C.E.)

2 Originally the Talmud was wholly oral, passed down through generations by word of mouth, discussion, and debate. It was put down in writing around 250 C.E. (Mishna) and 500 C.E. (Gemarah). The two words comprise the Talmud.

3 ShaS, which stands for Shisha S'darim, the six sections of the Talmud, each involving a different subject.

4 66

5 Hillel

6 Rashi, an acronym for Rabbi Shlomo Yitzchaki. He lived in the ninth century in Troyes, France. His unique Hebrew characters are known as Rashi script.

4. Film

1 Stephen Spielberg
2 Edward G. Robinson
3 Marilyn Monroe
4 Bette Midler
5 Elizabeth Taylor
6 Paul Muni
7 Lauren Bacall (she married Humphrey Bogart)
8 Harrison Ford
9 Alicia Silverstone

5. Codes

1 After the Talmud was written, every few hundred years rabbis and scholars condensed all of the laws and practices of Judaism into volumes for easy reference. These are known as the Codes.
2 A physician and scholar, he was the greatest Jewish philosopher of the Middle Ages.
3 Mishneh Torah (Study of the Torah). This codified hundreds of years of law and tradition and became the basis for future codes.

4 The Code of Jewish Law, edited by Rabbi Joseph
  Karo, a Sephardic rabbi, in the sixteenth century,
  became the definitive authority on traditional Jewish
  behavior, practice, and life. Rabbi Moses Isserles, an
  Ashkenazi rabbi, later added commentaries, which
  became part of the text.

5 Shulchan Aruch (prepared table) is the Hebrew name
  for the Code of Jewish Law. Mapat HaShulchan
  (tablecloth) is the name for the additional commentary
  of Rabbi Isserles.

6. Words for the Law and Practice

1 h

2 g

3 a

4 i

5 b

6 e

7 d

8 j

9 c

10 f

7. More Film

1 Kirk Douglas
2 Barbra Streisand
3 Peter Lorre
4 Woody Allen
5 Tony Curtis
6 Kevin Kline
7 Stanley Cortez
8 Dustin Hoffman

8. The Jewish Calendar

1 Lunar
2 The Bible
3 Twelve—unless it's a leap year.
4 Tishri, Heshvan, Kislev, Tevet, Shevat, Adar, Nisan, Iyar, Sivan, Tammuz, Av, and Elul.
5 Seven times in nineteen years. The rabbis made this adjustment to reconcile the lunar calendar with the solar calendar.

6 In the spring, before Passover.

7 Adar II.

8 Rosh Hodesh

9 At sundown. On the Sabbath, however, the day
begins eighteen minutes before sundown and ends
about forty minutes after sundown. Traditionally, the
Sabbath day ends when three stars appear in the sky.

10 Heshvan and Kislev.

9. Television

1 Mel Allen

2 Gertrude Berg

3 Peter Falk

4 William Paley

5 Tony Randall

6 Jerry Seinfeld

10. Dates and Events

1 g

2 d

3 h

4 j

5 n

6 o

7 c

8 f

9 q

10 i

11 m

12 a

13 b

14 e

15 l

16 p

17 k

11. Musicians

1 Benny Goodman
2 Theodore Bikel
3 George Gershwin
4 Irving Berlin
5 Al Jolson
6 Dinah Shore
7 Victor Borge
8 Jack Pearl
9 The Beatie Boys
10 Lenny Kravitz

12. Common Phrases

1 h
2 f
3 i
4 a
5 g
6 j

7 c

8 d

9 e

10 b

13. Stage

1 Zero Mostel

2 James Lapine

3 Sophie Tucker

4 Eli Wallach

5 Sarah Bernhardt

6 Maurice Schwartz

7 Fanny Brice

8 Wendy Wasserstein

9 Joseph Schildkraut

10 Arthur Miller

14. The Sabbath

1   The seventh day of the week.

2   The Bible (Genesis 2:3)

3   Rest (Shabbat)

4   Candles, wine, and challah.

5   She blesses the Sabbath candles.

6   He chants or recites the Kiddush blessing over the wine.

7   *Shalom Aleichem*

8   *Shabbat Shalom*

9   *Gut Shabbes*

10   With the blessing over the candles and the reciting of Kiddush.

11   Separation (of weekday from Sabbath).

12   Wine, specially branded candle, and spice box.

13   Officially at nightfall, but the lighting of the candles takes place at sunset, about forty minutes earlier.

14   To avoid desecrating the Sabbath.

15   According to some, to honor the two references to the Sabbath in the Bible; to others, to make enough light to avoid carrying a candle from room to room in a simple dwelling.

15. Words for the Sabbath

1 j
2 f
3 h
4 b
5 g
6 i
7 d
8 c
9 a
10 e

16. Comedy

1 Eddie Cantor
2 Jack Benny
3 Marx Brothers
4 George Burns
5 Jerry Lewis
6 Rodney Dangerfield
7 Carl Reiner

8 Stiller and Meara
9 Mel Brooks
10 Joey Bishop
11 George Jessel
12 Molly Picon
13 Lenny Bruce
14 Jack Pearl
15 Marcel Marceau

17. Birth

1 "Welcome, a boy!"
2 The first Friday evening after birth.
3 Covenant or circumcision.
4 The eighth day.
5 One who circumcises. A woman who circumcises is called a Mohelets. In the Bible, Zipporah, Moses' wife, circumcises her sons.
6 After the circumcision ceremony.
7 In the synagogue, usually the first time the Torah is read after the birth.
8 Redemption of the first-born son, on the thirtieth day after birth, by a Kohayn.

18. Funnymen

1 b

2 a

3 c

4 a

5 c

6 c

7 b

8 a

9 b

10 a

19. Words for Life Cycle Events

1 h

2 l

3 k

4 i

5 m

6 j

7 n

8 a

9 c

10 g

11 o

12 e

13 b

14 d

15 f

20. Composers

1 n

2 j

3 o

4 i

5 a

6 b

7 𝓍e

8 l

9 m

10 d

11 f

12 c

13 h

14 g

15 k

21. Bar Mitzvah

1 A coming-of-age ceremony for Jewish boys.

2 Son of the Commandment.

3 When he reaches the age of thirteen.

4 Recite blessings of the Torah, don tephillin/ phylacteries, and be counted in the synagogue adult quorum.

5 A coming-of-age ceremony for Jewish girls.

6 Daughter of the Commandment.

7 At the age of thirteen (in traditional synagogues, twelve).

8 *Bas* means daughter in Ashkenazi, *bat* means daughter in Sephardi.

9 Not generally, except in many Conservative and in Reform synagogues.

22. Sports

1 Hank Greenberg

2 Barney Ross

3 Sandy Koufax

4 Sid Luckman

5 Dick Savitt

6 Mark Spitz

7 Marty Glickman and Sam Stoller

8 Max Baer. Buddy was my brother. I won the championship by knocking out Primo Carnera in 1934.

9 Andy Cohen

10 Fred Lebow

23. Confirmation

1 A ceremony that takes place at fifteen or sixteen years of age that affirms, or confirms, faith in Judaism.

2 In the mid-nineteenth-century in Germany.

3 Shavuot/Feast of Weeks, when the Ten Commandments event is read from the Torah.

4 All Reform and Reconstructionist, many Conservative and a few Orthodox synagogues observe and celebrate.

5 Gowns are worn by confirmads. Flowers are carried by young women. Service participation includes cantatas and readings. Synagogue gifts are usually white Bibles and prayer books.

24. Words for the Temple

1 e

2 d

3 n

4 q

5 f

6 p

7 i

8 l

9 k

10 a

11 j

12 m

13 b

14 s

15 o

16 h

17 r

18 t

19 g

20 c

25. Marriage

1 *Chatuna*

2 *Chatan*

3 *Kalah*

4 A canopy under which bride and groom stand during the ceremony.

5 The new home of the bride and groom.

6 Two

7 The traditional ceremony consists of two parts, betrothal and marriage (these were originally separated by a year).

8 Generally two. In Orthodox ceremonies, a ring is given to the bride only.

9 There can be no diamonds (to avoid misjudging value).

10 In traditional ceremonies, the groom places the ring

on the bride's right forefinger, the finger of strength.
That is, betrothal is offered with strength and
accepted with strength.

11 Yes. Any item of value can be used.

12 The traditional marriage contract, written in
Aramaic, the language in which it originated.

13 Seven Blessings.

14 The groom.

15 Mazel Tov (good luck).

26. More Sports

1 Sylvia Wene

2 Benny Leonard

3 Victor Barna

4 Moe Berg

5 Henry Laskau

27. Funerals

1 As soon as possible, preferably before sundown the following day (unless the following day is the Sabbath).

2 Shomrim are people who are hired to clean and watch over the body until burial.

3 To show that we all are equal.

4 To wash ourselves of the differentness of death.

5 Roundness symbolizes the circle of life.

6 Seven days of mourning following the funeral.

7 Immediate family—parents, children, siblings, and spouses.

8 Tear clothing, cover mirrors, sit on low chairs, no leather shoes.

9 Prayer for the dead said for eleven months following the death to help the soul enter heaven.

10 Hebrew anniversary of the death.

11 A child mourns for parents for a full year. A spouse, the parents of a child, and siblings mourn for thirty days.

12 Before the one-year anniversary of the death. The duty to erect a stone begins the day after shiva.

13 Stones, signifying, "I was here."

28. Hall-of-Famers

1 j

2 a

3 g

4 b

5 a

6 c

7 a

8 e

9 g

10 i

11 f

12 h

13 b

14 d

15 g

29. Fast Days

1 Yom Kippur/Day of Atonement
2 More than twenty-four hours

3 Yom Kippur and Tisha B'Av (ninth day of month AV)

4 Taanit Esther (Fast of Esther)

5 Taanit Esther

6 Taanit B'chor (Fast of the First Born)

7 Tisha B'Av

8 a = 2 b = 3 c = 1

30. Rosh Hashanah

1 New Year (head of the year; beginning of the year);
   celebrated on the first day of the month of Tishri.

2 Leviticus 23:24

3 Yom Teruah (Day of the Sounding of the Shofar).

4 The challah of Rosh Hashanah is rounded upward,
   building up to look like a crown.

5 A ram's horn. In the Orthodox and conservative
   synagogues, it's not sounded on the Sabbath.

6 In the story of the sacrifice of Isaac.

7 The *Baal Tekiah* (Master of the Sounding).

8 *Tekiah* is the long sound. *Shevarim* are three separate
   sounds. *Teruah* is nine staccato sounds.

9 One hundred

10 *Tashlich* means "casting away." Traditionally, it

refers to casting away of sins at a riverside. It is observed in the afternoon of the first day of Rosh Hashanah. If the first day of Rosh Hashanah is the Sabbath, *tashlich* is observed on the second day.

31. Words for Prayer

1 k

2 i

3 j

4 m

5 q

6 o

7 a

8 n

9 s

10 c

11 b

12 e

13 h

14 l

15 d

16 t

17 g

18 p

19 r

20 f

32. Yom Kippur

1 The Day of Atonement (Day of Forgiveness, Day of Reconciliation).

2 Rosh Hashanah is the first day of the period called Ten Days of Repentance (or Return), and Yom Kippur is the last day of this period.

3 To atone for sins, ask for forgiveness, and pray for life.

4 *Shabbat Shabaton* (Sabbath of Sabbaths).

5 Translated as "All the Vows," it is the chant that begins Yom Kippur.

6 Neilah

7 At the end of Neilah.

8 *L'shana ha-bah b'Yerushalayim* ("Next year in Jerusalem").

9 At the end of the Passover Seder.

33. Authors

1 c

2 j

3 e

4 k

5 h

6 a

7 n

8 g

9 m

10 l

11 f

12 o

13 b

14 i

15 d

34. Sukkot

1 Feast of Booths (Feast of Tabernacles).

2 On the fifteenth day of the month of Tishri.
  (Leviticus 23:33–36–39)

3 According to the Bible, seven days. In practice,
  Orthodox and Conservative Jews (except in Israel)
  celebrate for eight days.

4 Holiday of Harvest or Ingathering (*Chag HeAsif*),
  and Season of Our Happiness or Joy (*Z'man
  Simchataynu*).

5 A temporary home erected to celebrate Sukkot. The
  roof is made from *s'chach*—natural growth, like
  cornstalks—which allow an opening through which
  one can see the stars and sky.

6 *Lulav* (palm branch), *etrog* (citron), *aravot* (willows of
  the brook), and *hadasim* (myrtle branches).

7 Join them as a bouquet, recite a blessing over them,
  and use them in synagogue processions and during
  the "Hallel" prayers.

8 One common interpretation is as follows: the *lulav*
  symbolizes the spine (body), *etrog* symbolizes the
  heart (emotion), *aravot* symbolize the lips
  (expression), and *hadasim* symbolize the eyes
  (perception). They all join to thank God for life and
  blessings.

9   *Shemini Atzeret* (Feast of Ingathering) and Simchat
    Torah (Rejoicing in the Torah).

10 By carrying the Torah around the synagogue in a
    custom called *hakafot* (circuits). Also by ending the
    reading of the Torah and beginning it all over again.

35. Words for Holidays

1   n

2   l

3   m

4   k

5   i

6   j

7   o

8   f

9   c

10 d

11 b

12 e

13 h

14 a

15 g

36. More Authors

1 Cynthia Ozick
2 Emma Lazarus
3 Meyer Levin
4 Ludwig Lewisohn
5 Samuel Yosef Agnon
6 Richard Elman
7 Isaac Bashevis Singer
8 Joshua Israel Singer
9 Shalom Aleichem
10 Saul Bellow
11 Hannah Senesh
12 Bernard Malamud
13 Harold Kushner

37. Hanukkah

1 Hanukkah is the Festival of Lights. It celebrates the victory of the Jewish people in the years 165–162 B.C.E. over the Syrians, who destroyed the Holy Temple.

2 For eight days, beginning on the twenty-fifth day of Kislev.

3 One cruse of pure oil was found in the Temple, and it lasted for eight days.

4 Chag HaOreem/Festival of Lights.

5 a. The father of the Maccabee brothers.

   b. The King of Syria.

   c. Son of Mattahias and military leader of the revolt.

   d. Another of Mattathias' five sons.

   e. Mother of seven children, she refused to submit to Antiochus.

6 It has three meanings. The first meaning is "hammer." The second meaning is a contraction of the first letter of four words, the call of Mattathias, "Who is like you, O Lord, among the mighty: Mee Kamocha-Bayleem-Adonai." The third meaning is "dedication," referring to the rededication of the Temple.

7 The special candelabra that has space for eight candles.

8 It is used to kindle the other candles in the menorah.

9 A spinning top inscribed with four Hebrew letters: "N," "G," "H," "S," signifying "A great miracle happened there." It is used to play a put-and-take game.

10 Potato pancakes, or *latkes* in Yiddish.

38. Artists

1 Marc Chagall
2 Maurice Gottlieb
3 Mane-Katz
4 Amedeo Modigliani
5 Camille Pissarro
6 Rueben Rubin
7 Shalom Von Safed
8 Ben Shahn
9 Raphael Soyer
(my brothers were Moses and Isaac)
10 Chaim Soutine
11 Arthus Szyk
12 Max Lieberman
13 Abraham Walkowitz
14 Max Weber
15 Larry Rivers

39. Tu B'Shevat

1 The Festival of Trees, celebrating the end of winter and the beginning of spring.

2 The fifteenth day of the month Shevat.

3 The "Tu" is used to represent the number fifteen, signifying the fifteenth day of the month. Although "Y" equals ten and "H" equals five, and together they also represent fifteen, they make the sound "Yah" which is the name of the biblical God. To avoid using God's name, "T", which has a number value of nine, and "V", which has a number value of six, are used to make fifteen—hence, "Tu".

4 Chamisha Asar B'Shevat, Fifteenth of Shevat, and Rosh Hashanah La-Ilanot (New Year for Trees).

5 About seventeen to eighteen hundred years, dating back to Talmudic times.

6 Eating special fruits such as dates, figs, and especially *bokser*, a hard bark with soft, sweet sap inside. Also, the planting of trees, especially in Israel.

7 Ashkenazi Jews often eat fifteen kinds of new fruit of the season on this holiday.

8 Sephardic Jews call the day Feast of Fruits. They often have a Tu B'Shevat Seder with four cups of wine and special readings.

40. Sculptors

1 Yitzhak Danziger
2 Sir Jacob Epstein
3 Chaim Gross
4 James Lipschitz
5 Louise Nevelson
6 Ossip Zadkine
7 Jo Davidson
8 Yaakov Agam

41. Scientists

1 Albert Einstein
2 Chaim Weizmann became the first
   president of the State of Israel.
3 Sigmund Freud
4 David Barnard Steinman
5 Benjamin Mazar
6 Admiral Hyman G. Rickover
7 Yigael Yadin
8 Emile Durkheim

9 A. A. Michelson

10 J. Robert Oppenheimer

42. Purim

1 Purim is a Jewish holiday which celebrates the
   Persian Jews' escape from a massacre. Haman, the
   evil prime minister, chose lots to decide when to
   attack the Jews.

2 "Choosing lots."

3 The Book of Esther.

4 By a special chant of the complete Book of Esther,
   called the *Megillah,* which means the "Scroll of
   Esther."

5 A special meal called *sevdat Purim* is prepared with
   hamantaschen which are cake pockets containing
   manna and fruits. It is common for children to reenact
   the Purim story by putting on a play.

6 A greggar, which is shaken to drown out the sound of
   Haman's name whenever it is mentioned during the
   Megillah reading.

7 a. The king.

   b. The first queen.

   c. Prime minister.

d. The king's guards.

e. Esther's uncle.

f. Haman's wife

g. The new queen.

8 They are three-cornered cakes eaten during Purim,
and are based on the shape of a three-cornered hat.

43. More Scientists

1 Ernst Chain

2 Charles Steinmetz

3 Casmir Funk

4 David Sarnoff

5 Edward Teller

6 Isidor Rabi

7 Arthur Kornberg

8 Otto Weinberg

9 Jonas Salk

10 Richard Feynman

44. Passover

1 Passover is a holiday commemorating the liberation of the Jews from Egyptian captivity.

2 On the evening of the fourteenth day of the month of Nisan.

3 Eight days.

4 a. *Maot chitim* (funds for wheat), a tradition of providing Passover necessities to the poor.

b. *Mechirat chametz* (selling the *chametz*), a ceremony designed to circumvent the restriction against owning or housing leavened products *(chametz)* during Passover. Leavened products are symbolically "sold," usually through the agency of a rabbi, in order that families may keep their leavened products without breaking Jewish law.

c. *Bedikat chametz* (searching for *chametz*), a tradition in which leavened products, usually pieces of bread are hidden, searched for, and found on the night before Passover, and then collected and burned the next morning.

d. *Taanit b'chor* (fast of the first born), a tradition in which the firstborn son of the family fasts on the day of Passover eve. This commemorates the death of firstborn sons of Egyptian families during the tenth plague.

5 *Chag Hamatzot* (Festival of Matzoh); *Chag HaAviv*

(Festival of Spring); and *Z'man Chayruteynu* (Season of Our Freedom).

6 In escaping bondage, the Israelites could not waste time baking bread and waiting for it to rise, so they prepared matzoh, or flat, unleavened bread. Matzoh subsequently came to represent freedom, and matzoh is thus a central symbol in the Passover celebration.

7 *Seder* means "order." It is the name of the essential ceremony of Passover, in which the various rituals must be observed in a specific order.

8 Haggadah, which means "telling."

9 Four

10 The three groups of Jewish people: Kohayn (Priests); Layvee (Levites); Yisrael (Israelites).

11 The middle matzoh is broken in half early in the Seder, with one half remaining on the table and the other half hidden. The hidden matzoh is the *aphikomen.* Usually, the children search for it and whoever finds it gets a prize.

12 None. Neither Moses nor Aaron nor Miriam is mentioned in the traditional Haggadah. The omission is intended to stress the idea that it was God, and not any human being, who was responsible for the Exodus.

13 For Elijah the Prophet, who, according to legend, visits every home during the Passover Seder and takes a sip of wine from the cup reserved for him. Elijah represents hope for the future

45. Passover Terms

1 c

2 d

3 a

4 e

5 b

46. Israel

1 David Ben Gurion

2 Abba Eban

3 Vladimir (Zeev) Jabotinsky

4 Herbert Samuel

5 Mordecai Manuel Noah

6 Golda Meir

7 Yitzhak Rabin

8 Theodore Herzl

9 Chaim Weizmann

10 David "Mickey" Marcus

47. Words for Israel

1 d

2 h

3 i

4 e

5 g

6 a

7 j

8 b

9 c

10 f

48. Shavuot

1 A celebration of God's giving the Torah (the Ten Commandments) to Israel.

2 *Shavuot* means "weeks."

3 Shavuot is celebrated on the sixth day of Sivan, the fiftieth day after Passover (Leviticus 23:15).

4 Two days, except in Israel and Reform synagogues, where it's celebrated for one.

5 *Sefirah*

6 *Z'man Matan Torahtaynu* (Season of Giving the
   Torah) and *Chag HaShavuot* (Feast of Weeks).

7 The tradition of studying the Torah, Talmud, and
   other Jewish sources all night long.

8 The excerpt describing the Israelites at Mount Sinai,
   with Moses going up the mountain and returning with
   the Ten Commandments.

9 The Book of Ruth.

10 Dairy foods.

49. United States Supreme Court

1 Louis D. Brandeis

2 Benjamin N. Cardozo

3 Abe Fortas

4 Arthur J. Goldberg

5 Felix Frankfurter

6 Ruth Bader Ginsburg

50. Lag B'Omer

1 A holiday celebrating the end of a plague. In Roman
times, Jews were not allowed to study the Torah. Rabbi
Akiba secretly taught many students. A plague struck
his students, and the day the plague ended became
Lag B'Omer.

2 The thirty-third day of the Omer. L is thirty, and G is
three. The holiday occurs on the thirty-third day after
Passover begins. The Omer is the fifty day period
between Passover and Shavuot.

3 With hikes and outdoor games.

4 Because of the plagues, weddings were not held until
Lag B'Omer.

5 Scholar's Festival, Outdoor Festival.

51. Political Figures

1 Bernard Baruch

2 Nahum Goldmann

3 Ronald Lauder

4 Edgar Bronfman

5 Herbert Lehman

6 Henry Morgenthau Jr.

7 Henry Kissinger

8 Golda Meir

9 Oscar S. Strauss

10 Judah P. Benjamin

52. Miscellaneous Words

1 t

2 e

3 i

4 p

5 o

6 k

7 b

8 q

9 f

10 a

11 d

12 n

13 g

14 r

15 h

16 s

17 c

18 m

19 j

20 l

BIBLIOGRAPHY

Ausubul, Nathan. *Pictorial History of the Jewish People.* New York: Crown Publishers, 1984.

Berkow, Ira. *Hank Greenberg: Hall of Fame Slugger.* Philadelphia: Jewish Publication Society, 1997.

Contemporary Authors Series. Detroit: Gale Research Company.

de Sola Pool, *David and Tamar. An Old Faith in the New World.* New York: Columbia University Press: 1955.

Encyclopedia Judaica. Jerusalem: Keter Publishing, 1971.

Patai, Ralph, editor. *Encyclopedia of Zionism and Israel.* New York: Herzl Press/McGraw Hill: 1971.

Goldman, Alex J. *The Eternal Books Retold.* New York: Pilgrim Press, 1982.

———. *Giants of Faith: Great American Rabbis.* New York: Citadel Press, 1982.

———. *A Handbook for the Jewish Family.* New York: Bloch Publishing, 1958, 1985.

———. *Judaism Confronts Contemporary Issues.* New York: Shengold Publishers, 1978.

———. *John F. Kennedy: The World Remembers.* New York: Fleet Press, 1968.

————. *Power of the Bible.* New York: Fountainhead Publishers, 1974.

Mazar, Ory N., editor. *Great Jews in Sports.* International Hebrew Heritage Series. Miami: International Book Corporation, 1969.

————. *Great Jews in the Performing Arts.* International Hebrew Heritage Series. Miami: International Book Corporation, 1969.

Lyman, Darryl. *Great Jews on Stage and Screen.* New York: Jonathan David, 1987.

Pearl, Chaim, and Brooks, Reuben. *A Guide to Jewish Knowledge.* London: Jewish Chronicles Publications, 1968.

Perl, Lila. *Molly Picon: A Gift of Laughter.* Philadelphia: Jewish Publication Society, 1997.

Ribalow, Harold U. and Meir. *The Jew in American Sports.* New York: Hippocrene Books, 1985.

Sachar, Abram L. *The Course of Our Times.* New York: Alfred A. Knopf, 1974.

Slater, Robert. *Great Jews in Sports.* New York: Jonathan David, 1983.

Siegman, Joseph M. *Jewish Sports Legends: International Jewish Sports Hall of Fame.* Philadelphia: Jewish Publication Society.

Turner, Jane, editor. *Dictionary of Art Series.* London: Macmillan.

Waxman, Meyer. *A History of Jewish Literature.* New York: Bloch Publishing Company, 1938.

Wollman-Tsamir, Pinchas. *The Graphic History of the Jewish People.* New York: Shengold Publishers, 1963.